Ashley Walters

Ashley Walters: A Tale of Resilience and Reinvention

Born on June 30, 1982, in Peckham, south-east London, Ashley Anthony Walters—also known by his stage name, Asher D—has lived a life that's as multifaceted as it is inspiring. Raised by his mother, Pamela Case, a local government officer, Walters grew up in a vibrant yet challenging neighborhood. From an early age, it was evident he had a flair for creativity and expression.

Early Life and Education

Ashley attended St. George's CE Primary School in Camberwell and later Pimlico School, where he excelled academically, earning good grades in all 10 of his GCSE subjects. However, his journey was not without its difficulties. In 2001, following a heated argument with a traffic warden, he was arrested for carrying a loaded modified air pistol and spent nine months in custody before serving a full 18-month sentence in a young offenders' institute. Reflecting on his troubled youth, Walters has credited his father's absence as a factor that led to his early brushes with the law.

Music Career: Rising with So Solid Crew

Ashley's love for music found its outlet when he joined the UK garage collective So Solid Crew, adopting the stage name Asher D. The group's second single, "21 Seconds," became a cultural phenomenon, topping the UK charts and cementing their place in the music industry. After the group disbanded, Walters pursued a solo career, releasing albums such as In Memory of the Street Fighter (2006) and The Appetiser (2008). His collaborations with other artists and independent labels showcased his versatility and passion for music.

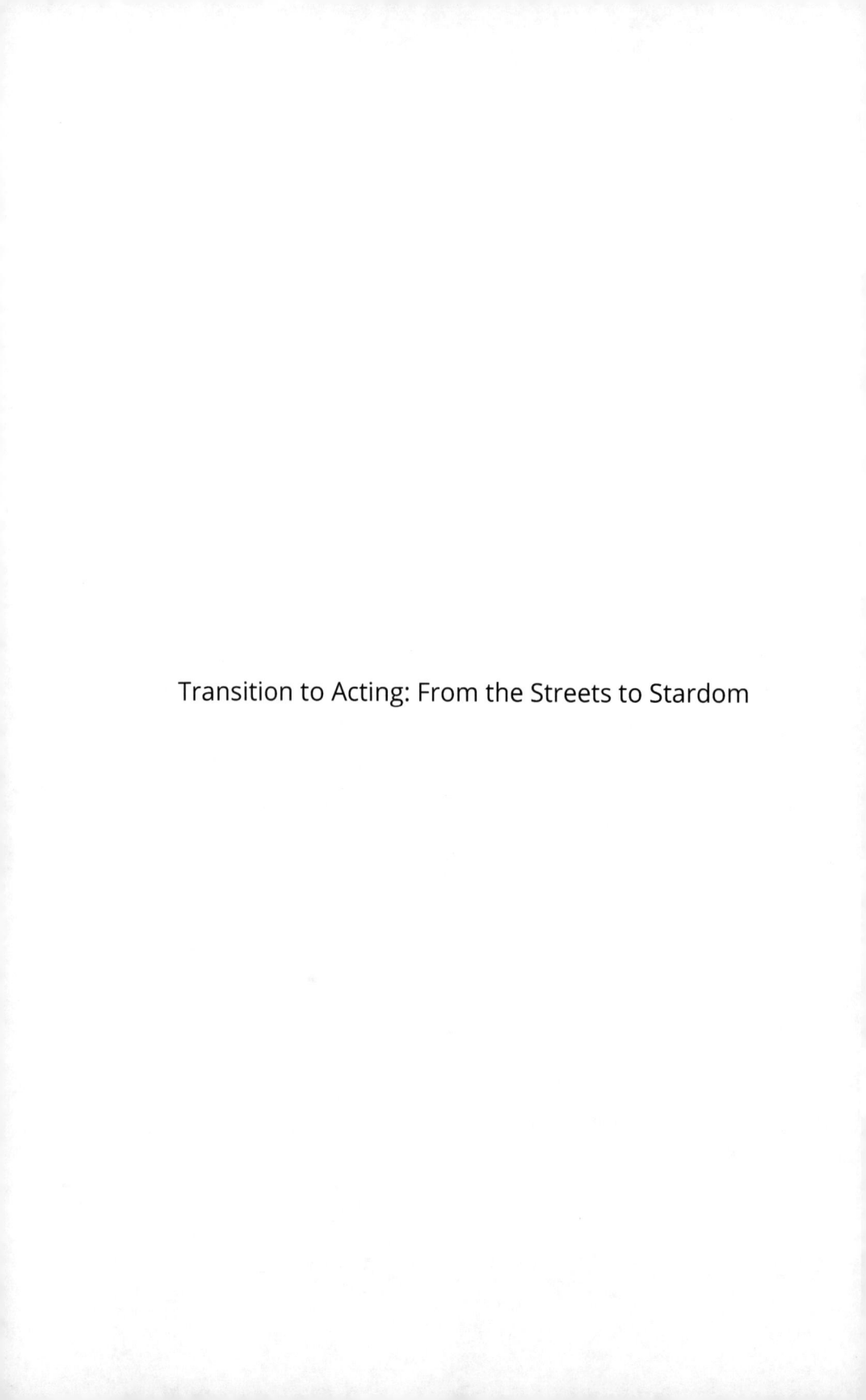

Transition to Acting: From the Streets to Stardom

While his music career soared, Walters also carved out a name for himself in acting. His big break came in 2000 with a role in the BBC drama Storm Damage. He gained widespread recognition with his portrayal of Ricky in Bullet Boy (2004), a powerful story of a young man trying to escape the cycle of crime. The role earned him the British Independent Film Award for Best Newcomer.

Walters' acting portfolio expanded with roles in international hits like Get Rich or Die Tryin' (2005) alongside 50 Cent and Life and Lyrics (2006). He ventured into television, appearing in popular British series such as Doctor Who, Silent Witness, and Holby City. His performances consistently displayed a remarkable range, from playing a jewel thief in Tuesday (2008) to his role as Michael in the BBC adaptation of Small Island (2009).

Top Boy and Mainstream Fame

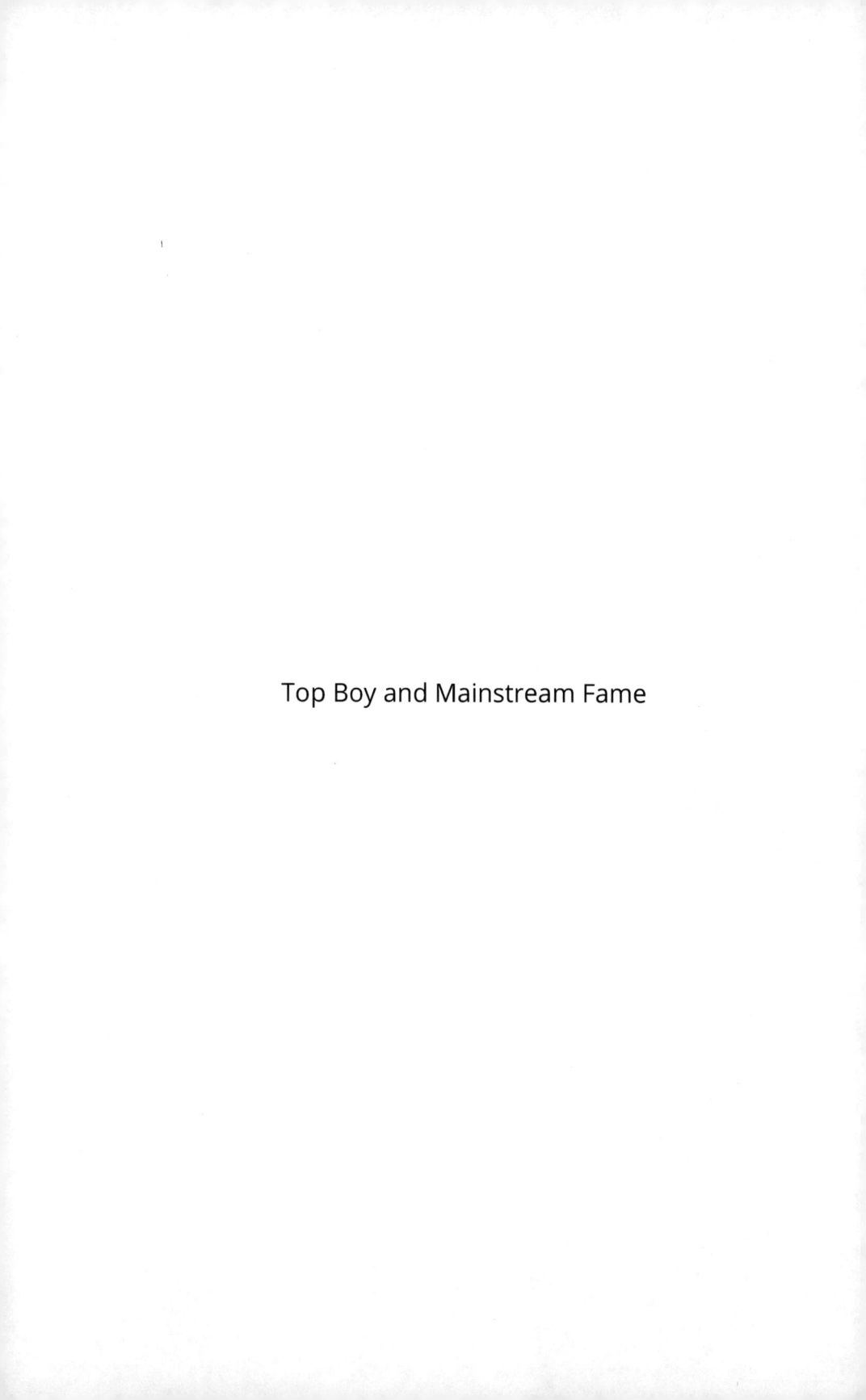

Ashley Walters achieved a new level of fame with his role as Dushane Hill in the critically acclaimed British crime drama Top Boy. Debuting in 2011, the series painted a gritty yet humanizing portrait of life in urban London. Walters' nuanced portrayal of Dushane resonated with audiences, making him a household name. After a hiatus, the show was revived by Netflix in 2019, allowing Walters to reprise his role and further solidify his place in British television history.

Beyond Top Boy: Creating and Leading

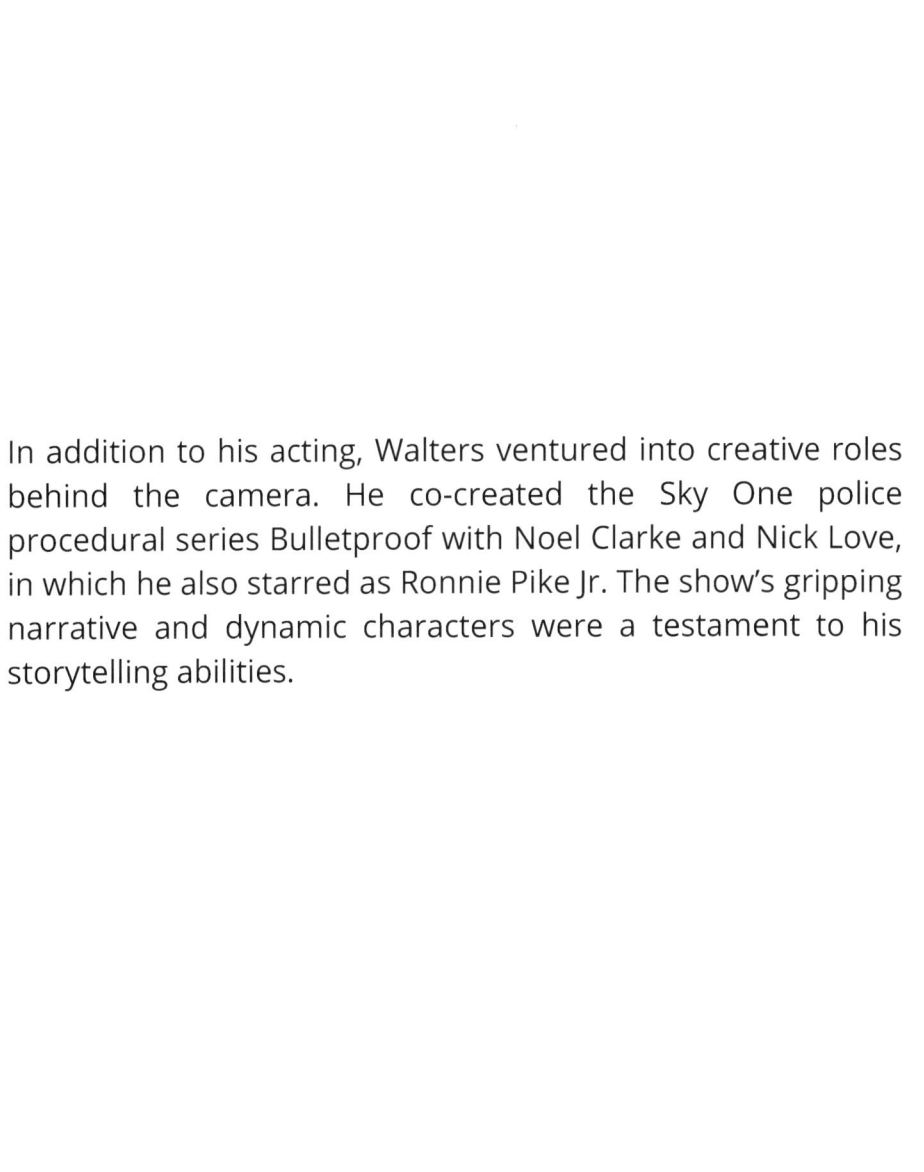

In addition to his acting, Walters ventured into creative roles behind the camera. He co-created the Sky One police procedural series Bulletproof with Noel Clarke and Nick Love, in which he also starred as Ronnie Pike Jr. The show's gripping narrative and dynamic characters were a testament to his storytelling abilities.

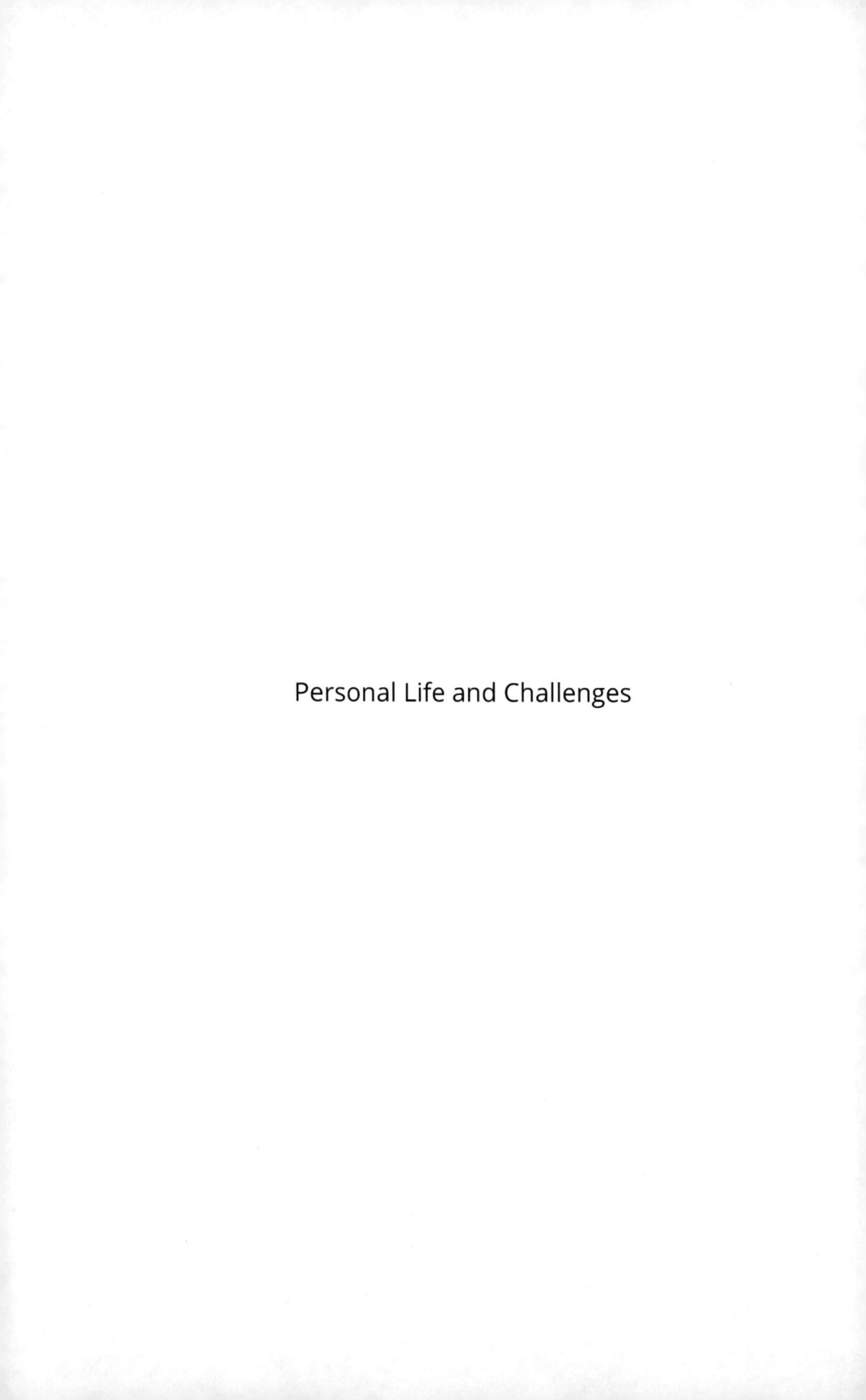

Personal Life and Challenges

Ashley Walters' personal life has been as dynamic as his career. He is the father of six children, four from a previous relationship and two with his wife, whom he resides with in Herne Bay, Kent. His journey has not been without controversy; Walters has faced legal issues, including fines for minor offenses. Yet, he has openly spoken about his past, using his experiences to inspire others to make positive changes.

An avid supporter of Arsenal F.C., Walters has also been politically active, signing a letter in support of the Labour Party's transformative agenda during the 2019 general election.

Throughout his career, Ashley Walters has shown an extraordinary ability to adapt, evolve, and thrive. Whether through music, acting, or storytelling, he continues to inspire with his resilience and dedication. His journey from the streets of Peckham to international stardom is a testament to the power of talent and perseverance.

With upcoming roles and projects, including the series Missing You and the film Adolescence, Walters remains a significant figure in British entertainment, reminding us all that reinvention is possible at every stage of life.

Ashley Walters' acting career continued to flourish in the 2010s, as he cemented his status as a prominent figure in British television and film. His breakthrough came with the iconic role of Dushane Hill in the crime drama Top Boy, a part that garnered significant attention and praise for his portrayal of a drug dealer navigating the gritty streets of London. His involvement with the show didn't end with his acting—he also became an executive producer for the later seasons, demonstrating his expanding role behind the scenes. The series gained even more widespread recognition when it was revived by Netflix in 2019, bringing new fans to the show and ensuring its place in the cultural landscape.

In addition to Top Boy, Walters had notable roles in other successful series. He co-starred in Bulletproof, a police procedural where he played the role of Ronnie Pike Jr., a National Crime Agency officer. He also co-created the series alongside Noel Clarke and Nick Love. The show became a popular hit for its compelling mix of action and drama. Walters also appeared in The Musketeers, Silent Witness, Cuffs, The Aliens, and Safe House, showcasing his versatility as an actor across a variety of genres.

On the big screen, Walters continued to make his mark with a diverse range of films. In 2016, he appeared in Billionaire Ransom, a thriller about a group of wealthy kids taken hostage, and later in Demain Tout Commence (2016), a French film where he played Lowell. His most recent roles have included the anticipated 2025 releases Adolescence and Missing You, continuing his prolific career in both television and film.

Outside of his career, Walters is known for his personal life, including his relationship with his ex-partner, with whom he has four children. He currently resides in Herne Bay, Kent, with his wife and their two children. Walters' struggles with his past, including his time in a young offenders' institute, have shaped his personal growth, and he has often spoken about how the absence of his father contributed to his early rebellious behavior.

Though he faced a few legal challenges over the years, including fines for various incidents, Walters has since focused on his career and family life. His advocacy for personal change and his work in both music and acting continue to inspire his fans. As a proud Arsenal F.C. supporter, Walters' influence extends beyond his entertainment career, as he is also involved in various charitable causes, highlighting his evolving role as both an artist and a figure in British culture.

Walters' continued success in acting and music, combined with his personal development and involvement in cultural and political discussions, marks him as a significant figure in British entertainment. His diverse body of work reflects his enduring appeal and capacity to engage audiences in both mainstream and independent projects.

Ashley Walters' career and influence have only expanded as he continues to navigate new professional endeavors. In recent years, he has embraced the role of mentor, guiding younger actors in the industry, particularly through his work as an executive producer. His commitment to helping develop new talent in both television and film has set him apart as someone who is not just interested in his own success, but in advancing the careers of others as well.

In 2020, Walters joined the cast of Gangs of London, a high-octane action series set within the criminal underworld. His performance as an unpredictable enforcer, juxtaposed against the show's intense action sequences and intricate plotlines, further solidified his status as a talented, multifaceted actor. The show received critical acclaim and helped introduce Walters to an even broader international audience, especially through its availability on streaming platforms like AMC+ and Sky Atlantic.

Additionally, Walters has delved into music production and collaboration, particularly in the genre of grime, where he has contributed both as an artist and a producer. His work within the grime scene, including collaborations with established musicians, has allowed him to remain relevant within the UK music scene, offering him another platform to engage with his fans beyond acting.

Walters' continued growth as an artist and public figure has led to increased recognition for his contributions to British culture. His versatility in both acting and music reflects a multi-dimensional approach to his career, where he can seamlessly transition from one medium to the next while maintaining his credibility and staying grounded in his roots. His role in developing new talent, especially in producing and mentoring, further demonstrates his influence in shaping the future of British entertainment.

In 2022, Walters also made strides in his charity work, becoming more vocal about the causes that matter to him, including supporting programs aimed at reducing youth violence and encouraging artistic development for young people. His involvement in charity initiatives has gained considerable attention, and he continues to advocate for better opportunities for disadvantaged communities, particularly in London, where he grew up.

As Walters moves forward, he remains committed to his craft, seeking roles that challenge him while simultaneously balancing his personal life. His ability to transition between genres and media, combined with his work behind the scenes as a producer, has positioned him as one of the most respected figures in British entertainment today. Whether on screen or in the studio, Walters continues to push boundaries and inspire those around him with his diverse range of talents and unwavering dedication.

Beyond his work in entertainment, Ashley Walters has increasingly become a prominent advocate for social change, using his platform to address important societal issues. His upbringing in challenging environments and his own experiences with adversity have driven him to support various initiatives aimed at improving the lives of young people, particularly those from disadvantaged backgrounds. He has often spoken about the struggles of growing up in tough neighborhoods and how the arts—whether through acting, music, or other creative outlets—provided him with a way out.

Through his involvement in initiatives such as mentoring programs for young actors, Walters has made it a point to encourage the youth to channel their energy into positive outlets. He has worked with organizations that aim to provide young people with the tools to succeed, whether through education, creativity, or career development programs. In 2021, Walters launched a youth-focused charity that offers workshops in acting, music, and business skills, providing a supportive environment for young people to express themselves and develop their talents.

In addition to his social activism, Walters' personal life has also been marked by his focus on family. A devoted father, he often speaks about the importance of fatherhood and family values. His role as a parent is something he holds dear, and he strives to set an example for his children, particularly with the lessons he's learned throughout his own career. Walters has been open about the pressures of balancing his professional and personal responsibilities, but he remains committed to being a positive influence in his children's lives.

His relationship with his partner has also been a key source of stability and support, allowing him to navigate the complexities of fame and personal life. Walters has spoken fondly of the importance of having a strong support system, emphasizing how his family has been a grounding force in his journey through the entertainment industry.

Looking ahead, Walters has expressed interest in expanding his career into other creative fields. He has mentioned an interest in directing and producing films that tell stories close to his heart, especially those that highlight the complexities of inner-city life and the challenges faced by marginalized communities. He is also passionate about creating spaces for diverse voices in the entertainment industry, advocating for greater representation of underrepresented groups both in front of and behind the camera.

Walters' vision for his career remains expansive, as he seeks not only to continue developing his acting portfolio but also to play a key role in shaping the future of British entertainment. His journey from a young, aspiring actor to a multifaceted entertainment industry figure and advocate for social change underscores the power of perseverance, growth, and giving back to the community.

In recent years, Ashley Walters has continued to diversify his professional endeavors, further cementing his place as a multi-dimensional figure in the entertainment industry. Notably, he expanded into producing and co-founded a production company with a focus on developing original content, particularly in the realm of film and television that speaks to the experiences of underrepresented communities. Through his production company, Walters has aimed to amplify diverse voices and bring attention to stories that might otherwise be overlooked in mainstream media. This work has contributed to his growing reputation as a creative force behind the scenes, not just in front of the camera.

His commitment to creating change within the entertainment world has also led Walters to serve as a mentor to aspiring filmmakers and actors. He has spoken passionately about the importance of mentorship, sharing his own experiences with industry veterans who guided him early in his career. Through his involvement in various industry initiatives, Walters has sought to foster an environment where young talent—especially those from disadvantaged backgrounds—can thrive and break into the industry on their terms.

In addition to his acting and producing work, Walters has become a vocal advocate for mental health awareness. Drawing on his own experiences of personal struggle, Walters has worked to reduce the stigma surrounding mental health, especially within the entertainment industry. He has used his platform to encourage open conversations about mental health and self-care, often sharing his personal journey of seeking help and the tools that have helped him maintain a healthy mindset. Walters has collaborated with several mental health charities to raise awareness and provide resources for individuals facing similar challenges, particularly among men, who are often less likely to seek support.

In terms of his ongoing acting career, Walters remains dedicated to taking on roles that challenge him creatively and personally. He has expressed a desire to explore more complex characters and stories that push the boundaries of his acting range. His work continues to be praised for its depth and authenticity, and Walters has received numerous accolades for his performances, particularly in roles that tackle social issues or portray multifaceted characters.

As his career continues to evolve, Walters has also shown a keen interest in expanding his influence beyond the UK, with several international projects in the works. His increasing recognition on a global scale has opened up opportunities for him to collaborate with artists from different cultures and backgrounds, further broadening his horizons as an actor and producer.

Through his various initiatives, Walters has become more than just an actor—he has emerged as an influential figure advocating for change in both the entertainment industry and society at large. His enduring impact on the industry, particularly in areas of representation, diversity, and mental health, ensures that his legacy will be felt for years to come. Walters' personal journey continues to inspire countless individuals, both in and outside of the entertainment world, proving that resilience, creativity, and the desire to make a difference can truly change the world.

Ashley Walters' influence has expanded beyond his work in entertainment and advocacy, as he has become an increasingly active figure in philanthropy and community engagement. Through his platform, Walters has worked closely with several charitable organizations, focusing particularly on causes that align with his own experiences and passions. His dedication to youth development and social justice has led him to partner with charities that provide support for disadvantaged young people in the UK, helping them find opportunities in education, employment, and the arts.

In his philanthropic work, Walters emphasizes the importance of mentorship, particularly for young people who may not have access to the same opportunities as others. He has often spoken about how mentors in his own life have played a crucial role in his success, and he is committed to paying it forward by supporting programs that offer guidance, skills training, and personal development to young individuals from marginalized communities. Walters' goal is to help these young people build the confidence and skills they need to navigate a world that often presents significant barriers for them.

Walters has also become involved in campaigns promoting positive masculinity, aiming to challenge traditional stereotypes around manhood. He has used his public platform to discuss issues such as vulnerability, emotional intelligence, and fatherhood. His openness in discussing his personal experiences with parenting has resonated with many, particularly as he navigates the challenges of fatherhood while balancing a demanding career. Walters has shared how his own upbringing and his desire to be a positive role model for his children have shaped his views on fatherhood, responsibility, and family life.

In terms of his professional aspirations, Walters continues to push for greater diversity both in the types of roles he takes on and the projects he chooses to be involved with. He has increasingly sought out opportunities that explore new genres, including international projects that allow him to engage with different storytelling traditions and expand his acting range. His desire to work on international co-productions is part of his broader vision of breaking down cultural barriers and fostering greater global collaboration in the entertainment industry.

As Walters continues to evolve in both his personal and professional life, he has also placed a significant focus on his own well-being. Aware of the pressures and challenges of working in a high-profile industry, he has become an advocate for work-life balance and self-care. His ongoing commitment to his health, both mental and physical, has influenced how he approaches his work and personal life. By being open about his own struggles and the steps he takes to maintain a sense of balance, Walters has inspired others to prioritize their well-being as well.

Looking forward, Ashley Walters shows no signs of slowing down. With a career that spans across acting, producing, mentoring, and philanthropy, his trajectory in the entertainment industry and beyond continues to rise. Walters has proven that true success is not just about professional accomplishments but also about making a positive impact on the lives of others. As he continues to navigate new challenges, he remains dedicated to creating spaces where others can thrive, break barriers, and achieve their dreams— just as he has done throughout his own remarkable journey.

As Ashley Walters continues to broaden his impact, his role as an industry trailblazer has become even more pronounced. He is now regarded not just as an actor, but also as a key advocate for cultural inclusivity, diversity, and representation. Walters has spoken out about the importance of seeing a range of stories, especially from underrepresented communities, being told on screen. He understands the power of media to shape perceptions and is committed to making sure that voices from various backgrounds are amplified. By championing projects that highlight marginalized voices and experiences, Walters has positioned himself as an advocate for real change within the entertainment industry.

Beyond his work within the film and television world, Walters has begun to take on more substantial roles behind the scenes. He has expressed a growing interest in producing and directing, with an aim to create content that reflects his values and experiences. As a producer, he has worked on projects that seek to inspire, entertain, and educate audiences while tackling pressing social issues. This move into production allows Walters to have more creative control, ensuring that the stories he helps bring to life have the depth and authenticity that he believes are so vital.

In his personal life, Walters has continued to focus on fostering meaningful relationships with his family, particularly with his children. He has spoken openly about how fatherhood has changed him, offering him new perspectives on life and pushing him to be the best version of himself. His desire to be a present and active father informs many of his decisions, from his professional projects to his commitments to charitable causes. Walters has made it clear that being a father is one of his most significant roles, and he is committed to being a strong, supportive figure for his children as they grow up.

His passion for social justice also remains a driving force in his life. Walters is keenly aware of the challenges that young people face, particularly those from disadvantaged backgrounds, and he has used his platform to advocate for better access to opportunities in education, employment, and community-building. His work with youth mentorship programs has allowed him to take an active role in shaping the future of the next generation, giving them the tools they need to succeed in a world that is often stacked against them. Through his personal and professional journey, Ashley Walters has demonstrated that success is not measured solely by individual accomplishments but by how one contributes to the collective well-being of others. His ambition to break boundaries—whether in his acting career, his advocacy for social causes, or his commitment to family—has set him apart as a multifaceted leader. As Walters continues to evolve, his legacy will undoubtedly be defined by his efforts to create opportunities, promote equality, and inspire others to take charge of their own futures.

As Ashley Walters' career continues to flourish, his influence extends beyond the entertainment world. He has become a vocal supporter of mental health awareness, acknowledging the importance of addressing psychological well-being in both personal and professional contexts. Walters has openly shared his own struggles with mental health, particularly the pressures of fame and the impact it can have on one's inner life. His willingness to be vulnerable has resonated deeply with his fans, and he has used his platform to promote conversations around mental health, aiming to reduce stigma and encourage others to seek help when needed. Walters has worked alongside mental health organizations, participating in initiatives to raise awareness and offer support to those struggling with similar issues.

In addition to his mental health advocacy, Walters has also become an active participant in initiatives that support environmental sustainability. Aware of the global challenges posed by climate change, he has lent his voice to campaigns focused on reducing carbon footprints and promoting eco-friendly practices. His growing interest in environmental issues has led him to collaborate with organizations that focus on conservation, sustainable living, and protecting natural resources for future generations. Walters believes that addressing environmental concerns is essential for the well-being of both current and future generations, and he has made efforts to integrate sustainability into his personal lifestyle, as well as his professional endeavors.

Despite his fame, Walters has remained grounded and focused on his roots. His connection to his community in London remains a cornerstone of his identity. He actively supports local initiatives that aim to uplift underprivileged communities, offering mentorship and championing programs that create opportunities for youth. Through various community projects, Walters continues to give back, ensuring that his success has a lasting, positive impact on those who may not have the same opportunities he had. His sense of responsibility to others is at the heart of his career and life choices, further solidifying his status as a role model.

On the horizon, Walters is poised to continue breaking new ground. Whether through his acting, producing, or advocacy, he is constantly striving to evolve and expand his influence. His commitment to creating meaningful, impactful work has ensured that his career remains relevant and inspiring, and his passion for storytelling has opened the door to new creative possibilities. Walters' dedication to his craft, his community, and his values ensures that his legacy will endure, both in the entertainment industry and beyond. As he continues to inspire with his actions, his story will undoubtedly serve as a testament to the power of authenticity, resilience, and the desire to make a difference.

Ashley Walters' journey into producing has marked an exciting new chapter in his career, allowing him to shape stories from behind the scenes. His experience as an actor has provided him with unique insights into the world of filmmaking, and he has used these perspectives to create content that resonates with diverse audiences. Walters has become increasingly involved in projects that reflect his personal values and experiences, including stories that highlight issues of social justice, empowerment, and resilience. His ambition to not only perform but to be a force of change in the industry through producing and directing further solidifies his place as a multi-faceted creative.

In recent years, Walters has also taken on roles in television and film projects that explore new genres and push creative boundaries. He has gravitated toward roles that challenge his versatility as an actor, stepping outside of his comfort zone to tackle complex and layered characters. Whether in gritty dramas or more light-hearted comedies, Walters consistently brings depth to his roles, demonstrating his range and commitment to his craft. His ability to fully immerse himself in different characters has earned him recognition and accolades from both critics and fans alike, cementing his status as a respected performer.

Moreover, Walters has expanded his influence globally. His success in British television and film has led to international opportunities, allowing him to collaborate with international filmmakers and actors. By branching out to global markets, he has brought his unique perspective and style to a broader audience, gaining recognition in international circles. Walters' work is not limited to the UK, and his involvement in international projects shows his potential to make an even greater impact on a worldwide scale.

Throughout his career, Walters has also placed significant emphasis on the power of collaboration. Whether working alongside established industry professionals or emerging talents, he understands that the best work often comes from a team effort. His respect for fellow creatives has fostered long-lasting professional relationships, and he has become a mentor and source of inspiration for many in the industry. Walters has been keen to pass on his knowledge to younger actors and filmmakers, encouraging them to remain true to their vision while embracing the collective nature of the entertainment world.

Looking ahead, Walters remains committed to using his platform for positive change. As he continues to expand his portfolio, his work will likely inspire others to take risks, push boundaries, and advocate for social change. His ongoing commitment to promoting diversity, mental health awareness, and sustainability serves as a reminder that art and activism can go hand in hand. With each new project, Walters adds another layer to his legacy, making sure that his influence on both the entertainment industry and society at large remains strong and meaningful.

As Ashley Walters continues to evolve as an artist and creator, his personal growth has mirrored his professional trajectory. Having faced various challenges throughout his life, Walters has developed a resilient mindset that has allowed him to navigate the ups and downs of the entertainment industry. His journey from a young aspiring actor to a successful producer and respected industry figure is a testament to his determination and adaptability. He remains grounded in his roots, never forgetting the struggles that shaped him, which adds depth and authenticity to the roles he chooses and the messages he advocates through his work.

Walters' commitment to giving back to his community is another key aspect of his character. He has used his fame and resources to support several charitable causes, particularly those that focus on youth development and empowerment. His involvement in initiatives aimed at providing young people with opportunities in the arts reflects his belief in the transformative power of creativity and education. Walters often speaks about the importance of mentorship and the role that support from others played in his own career, highlighting how valuable it is to invest in the potential of the next generation.

Despite the many accolades and recognition he has received throughout his career, Walters remains humble and deeply committed to continuous improvement. He is known for his work ethic and his ability to stay focused, constantly challenging himself to push boundaries and reach new heights. This dedication to growth is seen not only in his artistic endeavors but also in his personal life, where he strives to maintain balance and stay connected with his family, friends, and colleagues.

Walters' approach to his craft is defined by his passion for telling stories that resonate with real human experiences. Whether exploring themes of love, loyalty, betrayal, or redemption, he strives to create narratives that feel authentic and relevant. By drawing from his own life and the lives of those around him, he is able to imbue his characters and projects with emotional depth and nuance, making them relatable and impactful to audiences across the world.

In his ongoing career, Ashley Walters is likely to continue to be a driving force within the entertainment industry. His unique combination of talent, vision, and personal integrity ensures that he will remain a respected figure for years to come. With an eye toward future endeavors, including potential international collaborations and innovative projects that blend genres and media, Walters' legacy as an influential figure in the world of film and television is already well-established, and the best may still be yet to come.

Ashley Walters is increasingly recognized for his versatility as both an actor and producer, and his capacity to take on roles that challenge societal norms and highlight issues such as inequality, justice, and self-discovery. These themes, often central to his projects, stem from his deep understanding of the struggles that come with navigating complex social landscapes. His work continues to spark conversations about representation, providing insight into the lives of people who are often underrepresented in mainstream media. This makes his performances not only entertaining but also meaningful, allowing him to connect with diverse audiences on a deeper level.

Walters' impact extends beyond film and television. As an entrepreneur, he has made a name for himself in the business world, exploring various ventures within and outside the entertainment industry. His experience in producing and managing projects has equipped him with the skills necessary to expand his influence and pursue a variety of creative and business opportunities. In addition to his work as an actor, he has developed a keen interest in technology and innovation, particularly as they relate to the future of entertainment and media. Walters' forward-thinking mindset allows him to stay ahead of industry trends and adapt to the ever-changing landscape of film and digital content.

Despite his many professional achievements, Walters remains deeply connected to his roots. He is often vocal about the importance of staying grounded and maintaining strong relationships with his family and close friends. In interviews, he has frequently discussed the value of personal connections and the impact they have on his success. He credits his family and community for providing him with the strength and guidance to navigate both personal and professional challenges, and they continue to be a source of motivation as he evolves in his career.

Looking forward, Ashley Walters is committed to creating projects that not only entertain but also inspire change. Whether he is bringing awareness to social issues or helping to give a voice to marginalized communities, Walters sees his role as an artist as an opportunity to foster greater understanding and empathy among people from all walks of life. His ambition to use his platform for good remains a driving force in his creative endeavors, and it is likely that he will continue to challenge both himself and his audience with bold, thought-provoking work.

His growing influence in the industry, paired with his personal commitment to social impact and innovation, means that Ashley Walters' future in entertainment and beyond is filled with potential. As he expands his repertoire and explores new areas of creativity and business, Walters is poised to leave an indelible mark on both the entertainment world and the broader cultural landscape. His story is far from over, and his journey continues to inspire others to believe in their own potential for growth and success.

Ashley Walters' influence within the entertainment industry continues to evolve as he takes on new roles that reflect his growth both as an actor and as a person. His commitment to portraying authentic, multifaceted characters has made him a respected figure in the industry. Over the years, Walters has not only acted but has actively sought to shape the types of stories being told, advocating for more inclusive and diverse narratives. His approach to his craft highlights his belief in the power of storytelling as a vehicle for social change, inspiring both his peers and younger generations of actors.

In addition to his advocacy for diversity in media, Walters has become a role model for aspiring actors and creatives, particularly those from underrepresented backgrounds. He frequently speaks about his experiences in the industry, offering insights into the challenges and triumphs he has faced while navigating the entertainment world. By sharing his journey, he aims to empower others to pursue their dreams, regardless of the obstacles that may stand in their way.

Ashley's ability to adapt to new mediums and genres has also played a significant role in his career longevity. While he is best known for his television and film work, he has recently ventured into the world of digital media and online content. This shift reflects his interest in exploring the evolving landscape of entertainment, where platforms like streaming services and social media play a central role. Walters' adaptability ensures that he remains relevant in a rapidly changing industry, allowing him to reach broader audiences and engage with fans in innovative ways.

As a family man, Walters prioritizes his personal life, understanding that balance is key to maintaining long-term success. His relationship with his children and partner is a cornerstone of his life, offering him stability and perspective. He frequently expresses gratitude for his family's unwavering support, which has been a constant source of strength as he navigates the ups and downs of his career. Walters' dedication to his loved ones not only shapes his personal values but also informs the way he approaches his professional work.

Looking ahead, Walters is excited about future projects that align with his evolving vision of art and impact. He is particularly interested in taking on more leadership roles within the industry, whether as a producer, director, or mentor. By doing so, he hopes to continue pushing boundaries, creating opportunities for others, and building a lasting legacy that extends beyond his acting career. His passion for storytelling and his drive to make a meaningful difference remain at the heart of everything he does, ensuring that Ashley Walters will continue to inspire and leave a significant mark on both the entertainment industry and the world at large.

4o mini

Made in United States
Troutdale, OR
02/06/2025

28724714R00022